THE GREEK TEMPLES OF SICILY

THE GREEK TEMPLES OF SICILY

Alfred Dowling and edited by Salvatore Guglielmino

Published in 2025 by Connor Court Publishing Pty Ltd

The original edition appeared *The American Catholic Quarterly Review* in 1900.

Connor Court Publishing Pty Ltd

PO Box 7257

Redland Bay QLD 4165

sales@connorcourt.com

www.connorcourtbooks.com

Printed in Australia

ISBN: 9781923224940

Front cover designed by Maria Giordano

THE GREEK TEMPLES OF SICILY

Alfred Dowling and
edited by Salvatore Guglielmino

Alfred E. P. Raymund Dowling, a British Botanist of St John College, Oxford first wrote parts of this monograph in *The American Catholic Quarterly Review in 1900*. This has been edited and updated by Salvatore Guglielmino.

"You have heard that the city of Syracuse is the most beautiful of all the cities of the Greeks."

Cicero

Introduction

There are places on earth where time seems to move in layers rather than lines. Centuries do not pass but accumulate, like sediment shaped by wind and faith. Sicily is such a place. To stand before the temples of Akragas or Selinunte, their columns etched by sun and salt, is to inhabit a geography where mythology, philosophy, and history coexist. The island's stones speak in the languages of Greeks and Romans, Arabs and Normans, Byzantines and Bourbons. Yet of all these voices, it is perhaps the Greek that still resonates most profoundly. The Doric temples scattered along Sicily's southern coast remain among the purest expressions of classical form, and through them the island reveals not only its past but its enduring genius for synthesis, the meeting of the sacred and the sensual, the earthly and the divine.

When Alfred Dowling first wrote *The Greek*

Temples of Sicily at the turn of the twentieth century, he approached the subject not as an archaeologist or an art historian, but as a botanist. To modern readers, that may seem an unlikely vocation for a writer on the Hellenic world, yet Dowling's training lent him a sensitivity rare even among classicists. He saw the temples not as isolated ruins, but as living parts of a wider natural system, a landscape where flora, climate, and geology shaped the very texture of civilization. His was a contemplative gaze, attuned to how olive groves and limestone, wild thyme and coastal winds conspired to define an architecture that was both of the earth and beyond it.

Dowling wrote this essay for *The American Catholic Quarterly Review*, a publication better known for its theology rather than its travel. You can sense the age of his work from the very first page, where he describes his journey to Palermo from Naples by "a daily service of steamers". Today, of course, we have planes and Palermo's airport ranks among the largest and busiest in the world, a reminder of just how far both travel and time have carried us since Dowling's day.

Dowling's earlier significant work was *The Flora of the Sacred Nativity: An Attempt at Collecting the Legends,* published in 1900.

For Dowling, Sicily was not simply a field of stones; it was a moral and metaphysical landscape. For Dowling, the Greek builders of Sicily were not pagans to be dismissed, but early explorers of divine order, craftsmen who sought to express, through measure and proportion, the unity that Catholic theology would later articulate as the presence of God in creation. His writing belongs to a time when the boundaries between science, art, and religion were porous, when a botanist could write of architecture as a natural growth of the spirit.

It is precisely this integration of sensibilities that makes Dowling's work worth revisiting today. In an era obsessed with specialization, his synthesis feels radical. *The Greek Temples of Sicily*, in its original form, is part travelogue, part meditation, part scholarly report. Dowling's sentences unfold slowly, luxuriantly, as though written under the same southern sun that warmed the stones of Segesta. He moves from the scent of almond blossoms to the mathematical ratio of a colonnade with no sense of contradiction. For him, both are manifestations of the same order, the same Logos that St. John would name at the beginning of his Gospel.

As editor of this new edition, my task has been to bring Dowling's century-old observations into dialogue with our present understanding of Sicily's Greek heritage. Much has changed since he wrote. Archaeological excavations at Selinunte, Himera, and Akragas have revealed structures and inscriptions unknown in his time. Carbon dating, aerial photography, and digital modeling have transformed our comprehension of ancient construction methods. Yet, despite these advances, the emotional power of Dowling's account endures. His work is not outdated. It is timeless in the truest sense, because it perceives the temples as more than mere artifacts. They are, in his words, "prayers in stone".

In preparing this edition, I have sought to preserve Dowling's lyrical precision while clarifying certain passages obscured by Victorian idiom. Some of his theological reflections have been annotated rather than altered; others, I have expanded with reference to more recent scholarship. Where he wrote of "the Doric austerity of Girgenti", I have restored the modern toponym Agrigento, but retained his cadence. Where his botanical catalogues sometimes overwhelmed the flow of the narrative, I have moved them to the appendix, to allow readers to savor the prose without losing its scientific richness.

This is not a translation but an act of stewardship. An attempt to keep Dowling's voice alive within a contemporary frame. My goal is to let readers encounter both the original mind and the modern perspective simultaneously, as one might view an ancient fresco that has been carefully cleaned yet not repainted.

Sicily's Greek temples have always existed in tension between ruin and resurrection. The temples of Concordia and Hera Lacinia at Agrigento remain almost miraculously intact, their colonnades still commanding the valley as they did twenty-four centuries ago. Others, like those of Selinunte, lie broken across acres of wild grass, toppled by earthquakes and war, their fragments scattered like bones of an extinct order. Yet even in their disarray they retain a majesty that no restoration could improve. Dowling understood this. He wrote that "to restore the fallen temple would be to silence its most eloquent sermon," for decay itself is part of the sacred rhythm. The stones speak not only of endurance, but of transience, of beauty as a form of sacrifice.

In the decades since Dowling's travels, Sicily has undergone transformations he could scarcely have imagined: wars, migrations, the slow rebirth of its cities, and the modern rediscovery of its classical identity. The temples have become both archaeological sites and emblems of cultural resilience. They appear on postcards and currency, in films and tourism brochures, yet they remain profoundly local (anchored in the Sicilian psyche as symbols of continuity amid change). The shepherds who lead their flocks through the Valley of the Temples today trace paths not so different from those their ancestors walked when Dowling first visited. The almond trees still bloom in February; the Mediterranean light still turns the limestone gold at dusk.

For contemporary readers, Dowling's writing offers a way of seeing, an antidote to the hurried consumption of heritage. In an age when we capture the temples with a smartphone and move on, his patient attention invites us to linger. He teaches us to look at a column not as an object but as a gesture, a vertical translation of aspiration. His sensibility is at once Catholic and classical: he perceives in the Doric order a discipline of the soul, a geometry that mirrors the moral life. His Sicily is not only a landscape of ruins but a garden of contemplation.

If this book has a single argument, it is that the Greek temples of Sicily are not relics of a vanished civilization but living structures within the continuum of Mediterranean culture. They belong to no single epoch. The lines of their architecture run through later cathedrals, palazzi, and even modern design.

In editing Dowling's text for today's readers, I have resisted the temptation to turn it into an academic monograph. Its charm lies precisely in its hybridity: a scientist's observation infused with a mystic's reverence. My editorial hand has aimed not to polish away its idiosyncrasies but to let them breathe. The reader will find occasional archaic turns of phrase, but these are the flavor of a bygone English that once aspired to the cadences of scripture.

Alfred Dowling's *Greek Temples of Sicily* is, in the end, less a guidebook than a pilgrimage. It leads us through landscapes where faith and form converge, and where the silence of ancient stones continues to speak. As you read these pages, old and new interwoven, I invite you to imagine the island as Dowling saw it: the sea glittering beyond the cliffs of Agrigento, the scent of citrus in the air, and before you, the columns of Concordia rising like a hymn carved in limestone. In that moment, time folds, and the dialogue between the ancient and the modern begins again.

Catania, 2025.

THE
GREEK TEMLPES
OF SICILY

Most visitors to Sicily likely begin their journey in Palermo, the island's vibrant capital, which is well connected to mainland Italy by a daily service of steamers from Naples. Upon arrival, tourists are often captivated by the city's unique blend of comfort, an almost ideal climate, breathtaking landscapes, and the exquisite interplay of Saracenic and Norman architecture. The charm of Palermo is so persuasive that many visitors find themselves lingering far longer than planned, lulled by its beauty and tempted to forgo further exploration. The city's allure, much like the ancient Sirens' song, can seduce even the most determined tourist into settling in place.

Yet, true travel should serve a greater purpose, it should feed the mind as well as the senses. For those who allow their curiosity to lead them beyond Palermo's golden shores, Sicily offers an intellectual and cultural reward that few regions on earth can match. Within its compact borders lies a staggering concentration of historical richness and complexity. Every corner of the island whispers echoes of antiquity, inviting the thoughtful tourist to engage with a past that stretches from myth into history.

For the historically minded, Sicily is a living tapestry woven with threads from many civilizations. It stirs the memory with tales from Homer's *Odyssey*, the legends of Troy, and the vibrant pantheon of ancient mythology. Here, you can walk in the footsteps of Ulysses, gaze upon Greek temples like those at Agrigento, or visit the Roman mosaics of Piazza Armerina. The layers of history are continuous: from the glory of ancient Greece and the might of Rome, through the periods of Carthaginian, Byzantine, Arab, and Norman rule, down to the French, Spanish, and finally, modern Italian influences.

Even the geography of the island tells a story. Take, for example, the great headland at Palermo now known as Monte Pellegrino, or the Mount of Pilgrims. At its summit are believed to lie traces of the camp of Hamilcar Barca, the Carthaginian general and father of Hannibal. This solitary site, perched above the sea, can stir a thousand questions and memories of schoolroom histories. Who were the men who followed Hamilcar? What kind of people were they, who once left traces of their existence along the shores of Syria, the coasts of Spain and France, even as far as the British Isles and down to southern Africa?

The port of Palermo with a view of Monte Pellegrino, 1885. (Public Domain).

These people, known to us by many names, remain a mystery in many respects. The Romans called them Poeni; the Greeks referred to them as Phoinikes, supposedly after the palm trees near their settlements. Others named them Sidonians or Tyrians based on their cities, or simply Carthaginians, after their most famous colony. To the Israelites, they were the Canaanites, dwellers in the lowlands. But their true origin remains shrouded in uncertainty. What we do know is that they were among the earliest great traders and navigators of the Mediterranean. Homer himself described them as "skilled in trickery," hinting at a reputation for cunning commerce.

The Phoenicians brought with them a vibrant Eastern culture, including intricate musical instruments and fabrics dyed in the legendary purple for which they were renowned. In Sicily, as elsewhere, they left their mark not just through trade, but through their religion and ritual. On the island's many high places, they erected temples to their deities, most notably to the cruel goddess Astarte, or Ashtaroth, and to Moloch, whose worship demanded terrible sacrifices. These haunting remnants of a distant civilization add a layer of mystery and darkness to Sicily's otherwise golden and sunlit landscape.

It is not, however, the signs of Phoenician or Carthaginian occupation that we now propose to trace, although this might well be made the subject of a singularly interesting investigation and indeed, one worthy of serious reflection for modern nations who seem increasingly inclined to enshrine commerce as their highest ideal and national deity. Our journey now turns toward the legacy of a different people, a civilization of loftier aspirations and enduring beauty, one to which the human race owes a deep and abiding debt. The Greeks, with their unparalleled contributions to philosophy, art, and architecture, left behind in Sicily some of the finest examples of their architectural genius, temples that have withstood the passage of millennia.

From Palermo, the reach of modern rail makes it possible to visit the Greek temples of Segesta, Selinunte, and Girgenti (now Agrigento) with far greater ease than tourists of the past could ever have hoped. While the first two sites still require some forethought and a willingness to depart from the beaten path, the third, Agrigento, offers comfortable accommodation, including a hotel that rivals in charm and comfort the famed Hotel des Palmes in Palermo. The once remote marvels of classical antiquity are now within reach, and those who venture to them are richly rewarded.

For many, the chance to gaze upon a true Greek temple, not merely in the pages of a book or the halls of a museum, is a long-held desire. These majestic structures, though weathered by time and the elements, evoke a sense of sacred permanence. Their broken columns and timeworn stones speak more powerfully than any restored façade or reconstructed monument ever could. In their silent dignity, they remind us of the power of the ideal over the merely functional, and of beauty as a kind of truth.

Segesta[1]

Let us begin, then, with Segesta, whose magnificent
Doric temple stands alone on a rugged hillside
amid unspoiled countryside. The train carries us to
within five miles of the site, and the final approach
must be made on foot or by carriage, through a
landscape still bearing traces of its ancient past.
Segesta was long reputed to have been founded
by the descendants of the Trojan refugees, who,
according to Virgil and other classical sources,
settled in western Sicily following their flight from
the burning city of Troy. Whether myth or history,
the setting lends a mythical air to the place, with
rolling hills, quiet olive groves, and the scent of
wild thyme in the breeze.

---

1 Segesta, located in northwestern Sicily, Italy, and one
of the principal cities of the Elymians, a native people of
Sicily. Near modern-day Calatafimi, in the province of
Trapani.

The Doric temple of Segesta, Sicily, Italy

Though the journey by rail is a modest fifty miles, it demands patience, a slow, winding passage through mountainous terrain that offers ample compensation in its scenic beauty. As we round the base of Monte Pellegrino, we are reminded that even the route itself is steeped in legend and devotion. It was within a cave on this very mountain that the remains of Saint Rosalia, patroness of Palermo and niece of the Norman King William the Good, were discovered in 1664. Since then, the site has become a place of pilgrimage for Sicilians and travelers alike. Sir Walter Scott, moved by her story, immortalized her in verse:

"That grot where olives nod,
Where, darling of each heart and eye,
From all the youths of Sicily,
St. Rosalie retired to God."

These lines, from the opening canto of *Marmion,* capture the spirit of this rugged yet sacred landscape, where faith and legend blend into the very stones of the earth. The journey to Segesta, and indeed across Sicily itself, is thus not only a physical voyage but a pilgrimage through layers of time and meaning. With each step, we approach not only ancient temples of stone, but also the enduring ideals of harmony, proportion, and spiritual yearning that the Greeks sought to enshrine in their art and architecture.

Then, skirting the beauteous Bay of Castellammare for half its silvered circuit, the railway swings inland, cutting through fields and cliffs until you alight beneath the sheer, rugged front of Calatafimi. The town is known to modern Italians chiefly for the pivotal victory of Garibaldi in 1860, where he overcame the Bourbon forces during his bold campaign to unite Italy. Yet for us, the historical charm of the place lies in its deeper, more ancient association, as a boundary stone of the mythic wanderers whose fabled journey we first encountered in schoolroom Latin, through the stirring verses of Virgil's *Aeneid*.

From here, the modern tourist takes either mule or carriage and winds along a valley once sacred to memory, a land where even the rivers bear the legacy of the past. The Scamander stream flows gently through the gorge, so named by the Trojan colonists in poignant remembrance of the river near ancient Troy. The founders of Egesta, later known as Segesta, brought with them not just names and stories, but a culture, a longing, a deep-rooted mythology of home. Now, this place lies nearly as forsaken as Troy itself. Where once there was bustling life, temples, markets, and laughter, there is now only a haunting quietude. The stream that nourished its people also ran red with their blood when Agathocles of Syracuse, driven by greed and ambition, slaughtered ten thousand of its inhabitants to seize their treasures.

As we advance into this solemn valley, the temple of Segesta rises into view, first a suggestion, then a clear and commanding presence upon the left. To behold it for the first time is an experience etched forever in memory. It is, by general consensus and by its own sheer impact, the most powerful and harmonious of all Sicily's surviving temples. Its location alone is a marvel: poised at the head of a long, sweeping valley, set atop a natural plinth on the spur of a lone mountain, and perched at the edge of a deep precipice. The Greeks, with their unmatched instinct for aesthetic balance and spiritual resonance, could not have chosen a more commanding or poetic site.

All around are wild, forsaken heights, their nakedness only adding to the temple's nobility. The landscape is harsh, sublime, a chaos of cliffs, chasms, and rocky outcrops. Here, in this grandeur of solitude, the temple stands golden and silent, a sentinel of time. Its solitude is what strikes the heart: no sounds of village life, no bustle of pilgrimage or preservation. The stillness is absolute. The sky, sharp and cloudless, presses down with an unrelenting sun that seems to hold the valley in suspended breath. The air is heavy with the presence of ages, and as one gazes upon the structure, its Doric columns upright yet worn, the overwhelming sense is not just of ruin, but of the inevitability of fate, of the smallness of human ambition before the vastness of Time and the silence of the earth.

Climbing further, one glimpses Eryx (modern Erice) in the distance, like a crowned sentinel on the far western ridge. There once stood the famed shrine of Astarte, later Aphrodite or Venus, goddess of love and war, of fertility and the sea. From this height, the sunlit sea glints like hammered silver between the hills. The eye is drawn across a mournful and mysterious landscape, equal parts beauty and sorrow. It is a vision that stretches far and deep, a canvas on which nature has painted majesty and melancholy in equal measure.

All around is silence, save for the breeze that rustles the wild fennel and thistle at your feet. Occasionally, a butterfly wanders past, its gentle motion catching the light and casting reflection upon mortality, like the fleeting soul of the departed, as the local peasants still whisper, returning to its home. High above, hawks and falcons wheel in circles, ominous in their quietude. One treads here as in a vast cemetery of civilization. Every stone underfoot seems a relic; every breath, a borrowing from the past.

View of the historic town of Erice, Sicily, Italy.
(Creative Commons)

From one hill strewn with broken foundations, the ancient theatre of Segesta has been partly revealed, its tiers carved into the living rock. Once filled with voices, music, and ritual, it now seems suited only for the tragic, for performances echoing the gravity of man's rise and fall. Across a ravine, another hill rises sharply, crowned by the solemn temple, while beyond yet another crest lies the broken remnants of further edifices, each a ghost of greatness.

And yet, amid all this noble desolation, the spirit is not wholly subdued. For here stands enduring testimony to man's highest strivings, to reach upward, to commune with the divine, to make beauty an offering. The stones may crumble, but the aspiration does not. In the ruins of Segesta, as in the ruins of all great civilizations, we read not only a tale of loss, but a whisper of eternal truth: that in the fleeting arc of our lives, there is something within us that yearns toward the timeless, and strives toward the good.

Fortress of Erice, Sicily, Italy:
Remains of the ancient temple of Venus Erycina,
(*Wikipedia Commons: Norbert Nagel, Mörfelden-Walldorf, Germany.*)

The Doric temple that draws us here is among
the best preserved in all Sicily, owing largely to
the superior durability of the stone used in its
construction. Unlike many of its counterparts,
its surfaces are less worn by the centuries, and its
structure, though never completed, stands today
with a kind of rugged, dignified strength. It is
composed of thirty-six massive columns, six on
each front and rear façade, and fourteen along

either flank. These pillars, still unfluted, were evidently left in a rough-hewn state, lending the temple a more ponderous and solemn appearance than the refined elegance typical of completed Hellenic shrines.

At their base, the columns are nearly seven feet in diameter, and their height approaches five times this width, giving them a commanding yet harmonious proportion. The temple rises on a stylobate of four high steps, though these too remain unshaped and unfinished. Curiously, the cellar, or inner sanctuary, was never begun, which suggests that the temple was never consecrated, never used for religious ritual. Its dimensions, nonetheless, are imposing: the temple itself measures approximately 192 feet in length by 77 or 78 in width, and when the full breadth of the stylobate is included, it extends to nearly 200 by 85 feet.

What further elevates this monument is the survival of much of its entablature, nearly intact around the entire perimeter. The architrave, formed of great monolithic stone blocks that span the gaps between columns, has been sensibly reinforced in recent times by iron rods, a commendable act of preservation by the modern government. This measure ensures that this noble relic, even in its unfinished state, remains a source of wonder and instruction to generations of tourists.

Scholars estimate that the temple's construction began sometime before 409 B.C., a date coinciding with the long and troubled period of hostility between Segesta and its powerful Greek rival, Selinus (Selinunte), more than fifty miles to the south. These ongoing hostilities, particularly Segesta's appeals for external aid, set the stage for both the Carthaginian invasion and, earlier, the ill-fated Athenian expedition of 413 B.C., both of which altered the course of Sicilian history. These conflicts likely interrupted and ultimately halted construction of the temple. Yet Segesta managed to endure, even long after Selinus was razed by the Carthaginians, surviving as a town well into the Roman period.

Indeed, it is from Roman sources that we get a vivid picture of life in Segesta, particularly from Cicero, whose impassioned speech against the corrupt governor Verres offers both history and drama.[2] Segesta, he tells us, possessed a statue of Artemis (or Diana), cast in bronze, revered not only for its religious significance but also for the artistry of its craftsmanship. Even enemies, Cicero writes, regarded it as sacred and beautiful, "worthy of being religiously worshipped".

This statue had once been plundered by the Carthaginians, but was later restored to the city by Publius Scipio Africanus following the fall of Carthage. Its return sparked joyous celebration in Segesta, it was a symbol of civic pride, of cultural continuity, of divine favor returned. It stood in honor once more, admired by citizens and strangers alike. Cicero, serving as quaestor in Sicily, recalls that it was the very first treasure shown to him on his arrival.

But that joy was short-lived. The infamous Gaius Verres, whose name has become a byword for avarice and impiety, demanded the statue for himself. The Segestan magistrates, faced with his threats, resisted as long as they could. They pleaded, they protested. Yet the pretor's tyranny

2   "In Verrem" ("Against Verres") is a group of speeches by Cicero from 70 BC. He gave them during a trial to prove that Gaius Verres, who used to be the governor of Sicily, was guilty of being corrupt and stealing from the people there.

knew no bounds. He oppressed the city with such severity that finally, fearing further violence, they relented. Still, no citizen of Segesta could be found willing to commit the desecration of removing the statue. It was only by importing mercenaries from Lilybaeum (modern Marsala) that Verres was able to fulfill his sacrilege.

Thus did Segesta, once again, suffer humiliation and loss. Her history, marked by struggle and misfortune, seems tragically consistent. The very name "Egesta", when rendered into Latin, echoes the word for poverty or waste, and the Romans themselves found this implication so ill-omened that during the First Punic War, the town formally changed its name to Segesta. But the misfortunes did not end with the name.

Today, Segesta's fate remains visible in the forlorn state of its few remaining inhabitants. The town is little more than a memory, a scattered handful of ruined homes and rough farmsteads amidst the grandeur of its classical bones. The poverty, the neglect, and the air of abandonment only serve to heighten the contrast with the noble aspirations of the people who once laid the foundations of its temple.

Still, Segesta moves the heart not merely because of its tragedy, but because of its enduring witness to a past that reached toward the sublime. It is a place where stone and silence speak volumes, where broken columns bear not just the weight of architecture but of memory, of history, of spiritual yearning. Here, we stand face to face with the noblest ambitions of ancient humanity, ambitions that time, though it may erode, has not erased.

Although the remains at Selinus (Selinunte) are simply tremendous in scale, presenting what is perhaps the largest single mass of classical ruins in all Europe, they do not at first yield the aesthetic satisfaction one might expect. This is not the serene perfection of Paestum or the balanced grace of the Parthenon, but instead an overwhelming chaos, a sea of shattered columns, collapsed cellae, and tumbled entablatures. No complete column remains standing, and it requires a considerable effort of the imagination to mentally reconstruct the majesty that once crowned these hills.

The site is divided between two principal heights. On one elevation, to the east, rise the ruins of three vast temples and a smaller shrine, the latter a temple in antis, consisting only of a cella with projecting columns at the entrance. On the other hill, to the west, the ancient Acropolis presides, where another three large temples once stood. Separating these plateaus is a deep valley, through which a modest stream flows toward the sea. This little watercourse, now choked with reeds and stagnant pools, once formed the harbor of the city, still remembered in the name Marinella di Selinunte. According to tradition, it was Empedocles of Agrigentum[3] who oversaw the drainage and improvement of this basin, a fitting act for the philosopher-scientist whose mind spanned both metaphysics and engineering. A monument once raised here in his honor has since been disassembled, its fragments now housed in the Palermo Museum.

3   Empedocles (around 492 to 430 BC) was a Greek thinker from a city called Agrigentum (also known as Acragas) in Sicily. He believed that everything in the world is made from four basic things, water, earth, air, and fire, which he called the "roots" of all matter.

Archaeological site of Selinunte (Sicily, Italy) - Walls
(2022, Benjamin Smith, Wikipedia Commons)

Selinus stood proudly upon two natural platforms, created by mountain spurs descending toward the sea. The western spur supported the Acropolis, its town quarters nestled just behind, all enclosed within ancient walls. The eastern spur, in contrast, was devoted wholly to the sacred. The temples alone occupying this high ground, unaccompanied by any secular structures. The first impression upon arriving is one of immense confusion, as though some cosmic force had swept across the landscape and toppled these colossal relics like a careless hand brushing chess pieces from a board.

Here lie sixty massive columns, flung to earth as though in defiance of time itself. Their scale astonishes, the locals call them *i pilieri dei Giganti*, the "Pillars of the Giants". The most significant of these temples, thought to have been dedicated to Hercules, had seventeen columns on each side and a double portico at the front. On the northern side, the columns have fallen outward, their individual drums still arranged in an almost orderly fashion, one atop another like vertebrae from some Titan's spine. Beyond them lie immense architraves, friezes, and cornices, forming a kind of fractured architectural script, waiting for the learned hand to decode their significance.

On the southern side, however, the collapse has been more violent: the columns have toppled inward, crashing through the cella, crushing it beneath the weight of their collapse. Some of the shafts were monoliths, but more often they were composed of six individual drums, precisely fitted and once held together by bronze dowels. These columns reached a height of twenty-eight feet, and, unlike the standard Doric form which typically features twenty flutes, the portico columns here have sixteen, and the rest eighteen, suggesting perhaps a regional or early stylistic variation.

Most curious of all is the narrowness of the cella,[4] or inner sanctuary, in proportion to the overall size of the temple. While the full structure measured 230 feet in length by 88 in breadth, the cella was just 131 feet long by 30 feet wide, giving the impression of an elongated outer shell enclosing a more modest spiritual core. The entire edifice rested on a stylobate of four steps, with an additional nine steps at the entrance. This shrine, the oldest of all the Selinuntine temples, is believed to have been erected soon after the city's founding, around 628 B.C., and thus represents some of the earliest extant Doric architecture in Sicily.

Preserved in the Museum of Palermo[5] are important fragments of this very temple, including parts of the entablature and three of the metopes, those square sculpted panels that adorned the frieze. Replicas of these metopes are housed in the British Museum, where they are valued not

---

4   The cella was usually a plain, windowless rectangular room with a doorway or open entrance at the front, often hidden behind a row of columns. In bigger temples, the cella was often split into three parts — a main central area (called the nave) with two side sections (aisles), separated by rows of columns.

5   Antonino Salinas Museum in Palermo

for their beauty but for their historical and artistic significance. They are strikingly archaic, almost primitive in execution, yet animated by a vigorous energy and the earnestness of early artistic struggle. They do not follow the polished conventions of later classical sculpture; instead, they represent an emergent style, seeking to express movement, emotion, and mythic action while still tethered to rigid traditions.

Their exaggerated limbs and stylized features may strike modern viewers as grotesque, especially when seen up close. Yet, much like the Gothic sculptures perched high on cathedral spires, these metopes were likely more graceful and coherent when viewed in their original setting, elevated above the ground, softened by distance and bathed in sunlight. The scenes carved upon them draw from mythological narratives: one shows a charioteer crowned by Victories; another captures the dramatic moment when Perseus beheads Medusa as Athena looks on; and a third depicts Heracles grappling with the serpentine Cecrops. Together, they embody the bold and violent iconography characteristic of early temple art.

These stones, now silent, once spoke of glory and

faith, of human triumph and divine spectacle. They were meant to inspire awe, to elevate the soul, and to enshrine the values of a people at the edge of the known world. Greeks standing firm at the threshold between Europe and Africa, between West and East.

Metope From the Temple at Selinus,
(Antonino Salinas Museum in Palermo)

Next we come to Girgenti (Agrigento), home of the Valley of the Temples, or perhaps explore the Phoenician legacy at Motya and the splendid mosaics of Piazza Armerina. This colossal northern temple believed to have been dedicated to Apollo stands as one of the most grandiose testaments to ancient Hellenic ambition on Sicilian soil. Though never completed, its scale alone compels reverence: 371 feet in length by 177 in width, it exceeds in length all other temples in Sicily and ranks among the most massive Grecian sanctuaries ever attempted. And yet, it remains a ghost of a vision unfulfilled, its columns unfluted, its roof never placed, and blocks still lying half-hewn in the abandoned quarries.

Its architectural plan marks a significant departure from the norm in Selinuntine design. Whereas most of the temples here are hexastyle, having six columns at the front, this temple was built on an octastyle plan: eight columns on the façade and rear, with seventeen on each side, for a total of forty-six. This configuration, along with its immense proportions and unfinished state, lends it a haunting grandeur, the sublime pathos of something never quite brought to life.

Agrigento, Valley of the Temples
(Photo taken by Maarten Sepp, Wikipedia Commons)

The columns once soared fifty-three feet high, tapering from a base thirteen and a half feet in diameter to a slender six or eight feet near the top. Now, these towering drums lie in silent ruin, some still stacked where they fell, others strewn across the ground as if hurled by an offended god. Their collapse, likely wrought by an earthquake, that relentless adversary of Mediterranean antiquity, has left behind a monumental wreck: a sprawling, sublime chaos of stone, at once a testament to the grandeur and the vulnerability of classical civilization.

It is here, amid the desolation, that the spirit of Selinus seems most vividly alive. One walks not merely among relics, but among dreams arrested in stone, visions of order and divinity never fully realized. As one surveys the fragments, the towering column shafts, the shattered capitals, the entablatures and architraves scattered across this sacred ground, a quiet yearning stirs: a longing for the resurrection of these marvels. In an age of engineering mastery and scholarly devotion, might not some portion of this hallowed grove be raised again? Not to indulge antiquarian pride, but to honor the genius and toil of those who first gave shape to such magnificence.

To the south, on the opposite plateau, the temple of Hera stands in equal eloquence, if quieter in tone. Though smaller than that of Apollo, and more severely ruined, it speaks not of incompletion but of proud duration and dignified fall. Fifteen columns lined each flank, with six at front and rear, rising from a stylobate of four steps, approached by an imposing flight of eleven. Of its once-powerful peristyle, only three columns stand erect, solemn witnesses to the passage of centuries and the indifference of time.

Yet this temple has left behind a more vivid artistic legacy than any other at Selinus: the metopes now housed in the Palermo Museum, where Greek mythology and Sicilian craftsmanship converge at their zenith. The scenes they depict: Athena striking down Enceladus, Heracles battling the Amazon queen Hippolyta, Zeus and Hera enthroned on Mount Ida, and Artemis confronting the doomed Actaeon. They all evoke an age when mythology was not mere story but the language of cosmic truth, and sculpture its highest expression.

Unlike the primitive vigor of the metopes from the Heraclean temple, these later works show an evolution in form, balance, and anatomical understanding. Though not equal to the masterpieces of Attica[6], there is here a refined artistic intention, a striving toward harmony, even if not yet fully achieved. Of particular interest is the technique of inlaying female flesh with

---

6   Attica is an ancient district of Greece where its chief city
      was Athens, and is bordered by the Aegean Sea.

white marble, a device that must have enhanced the naturalism of the figures when seen in their original, elevated setting.

Still, there remains something curiously unliberated in their execution, a stiffness in movement, a hesitancy in the drapery, a sense of sculptors conscious of innovation, but still reverent of tradition. The contrast between the archaic metopes of Heracles and the later, more sophisticated ones of Hera reveals a remarkable arc of artistic progression, made all the more poignant by its sudden interruption. Had Selinus not fallen to the Carthaginians in 409 BC, who knows what aesthetic achievements might have arisen from these hills?

As the sun begins to dip behind the western ridge, casting long shadows across the ruined sanctuaries, one is struck anew by the poignant beauty of Selinus. Unlike the neatly preserved ruins of Athens or Rome, here is a site that demands imagination, interpretation, and emotional investment. It is a city of echoes, a place where each stone seems to ask the visitor not merely to admire, but to remember and perhaps, to mourn.

Shall we now continue on to Agrigentum (modern

Agrigento) and explore the splendor of the Valley of the Temples, where the sacred legacy of ancient Akragas stands in haunting majesty?

The approach to Girgenti, modern Agrigento, the ancient Akragas, is thus not only a geographical transition but a spiritual one. Here, from the moment one glimpses the Valley of the Temples, with its ruined colonnades silhouetted against the southern sun, there begins a kind of pilgrimage into the soul of Magna Graecia. No ruin here lies mute; each speaks with the authority of an age when city-states were sanctuaries of gods, art, and memory.

As the road winds up the rising slopes, each turn unveils a fragment of ancient glory. Here, embedded in the golden earth, lie the remnants of one of the wealthiest cities of the Greek world. Empedocles[7], the philosopher and proto-scientist, who once walked these hills; Pindar praised its beauty and abundance; and Diodorus Siculus[8], its

---

7   Empedocles (born around 490 BC in Acragas, Sicily, and died around 430 BC in Greece) was a well-known thinker of ancient times. He was a philosopher, a political leader, a poet, a spiritual teacher, and someone who studied how the body and nature work.

8   Diodorus Siculus was an ancient Greek historian from Sicily who lived in the 1st century BC. He's best known for writing

native historian, spoke of two hundred thousand citizens and a life of splendour. This was a city whose horses triumphed at Olympia, and whose temples rivalled those of Athens in both scale and magnificence.

At the heart of Akragas lies its sacred crown: the Valley of the Temples, misnamed, for it is no valley at all, but a long rocky ridge running parallel to the sea, across which rise one after another the noblest monuments of ancient Sicilian piety and pride. Here stand the remains of ten or more major temples, dedicated to the Olympian gods, all facing east as if to greet Apollo himself with the rising sun. Time, earthquakes, and war have done their worst, but what remains is enough to stir the modern soul to awe.

The most complete and majestic of them is the Temple of Concord, so well-preserved that one may walk beneath its entire colonnade and imagine the full ceremony of ancient ritual. It stands serene, almost untouched by time, thirty-

---

a huge history book called *Bibliotheca Historica* (or "Historical Library"), which tried to tell the full story of the world from mythical times up to his own day. His work gives us a lot of valuable information about ancient cultures, including the Egyptians, Greeks, and Romans.

four Doric columns still upright, their capitals intact, their entablature still commanding the eye. For centuries it survived by accident, converted into a Christian church in the early Middle Ages, and thus spared the fate of its neighbors. The very name Concord is a romantic guess by Renaissance antiquarians; the true deity to whom it was dedicated remains unknown.

Temple of Concordia, Agrigento, Sicily
(Author Ludvig14, Wikipedia Commons)

Nearby, but more deeply ruined, lies the Temple of Heracles, likely the oldest in the city, with eight columns still erect, heavily weathered yet heroic in stature. It bears witness to a time when the Dorian settlers, fresh from their voyage, raised monuments to the protector of toil and courage. The stylobate upon which it rests shows the familiar triple-stepped platform, but the interior has long collapsed, and its massive drums lie tumbled in picturesque disorder.

The Temple of Zeus Olympios, however, is the most ambitious in scale. Begun after the victory over Carthage in 480 BC, it was to be a declaration of power, the largest temple in the Greek world. But it was never completed. Its enormous, fluted columns, over sixty feet tall if finished, lay fragmented, and the singular feature of Atlases, or giant male figures once supporting the entablature, remains only in parts. One such Titan lies on the ground still, face to the heavens, worn by time but unmistakably powerful, a symbol of human effort arrested by fate.

Temple of Heracles, late 6th century BC. Were newly erected 8 from the original 38 columns in Doric style. Archaeological Park of Agrigento.

(Wikipedia Commons)

And so the temples stretch along this ridge, some isolated, some grouped, their dedications known or guessed: Hera, Hephaestus, Castor and Pollux, and others lost to record. All were built in that golden century between the 6th and 5th centuries BC, when the city was at its height. Their stones were quarried from the ridge itself; the same shell-laden rock upon which they rest was carved to yield their massive blocks. Thus the temples and the earth are one: a continuity of form, color, and meaning.

There is a strange harmony in Agrigento between ruin and resilience. Though the city was sacked, first by Carthage, then by Rome, and much later ravaged by Saracens and Normans, its spirit seems never extinguished. The modern town rises just above the temples, detached yet still aware of the sacred ground below. Its churches and narrow streets betray no grandeur, but the panorama it commands is unmatched.

Stand at Rupe Atenea[9], the rocky summit once crowned by the Temple of Athena, and look to the south. Below, the great temples lie spread across the land like the pages of an open book. Beyond them, the earth slopes gently toward the sea, its surface flashing blue and white in the sun. To the west, olive groves and almond trees dissolve into the dry, rolling hills. To the east, the coastline curves softly toward Gela and the far-off outlines of Syracuse. Behind you, the highlands rise in quiet majesty, their silence echoing through time.

What, then, does Agrigento teach us? Perhaps that civilization is a palimpsest, layered, weathered, and enduring. That beauty, once shaped in stone, never fully vanishes. And that the human drive to build, for the gods, for memory, for the future, is one of our most profound and lasting aspirations.

We continue our ascent past these noble relics, and soon we find ourselves before the best-preserved temple in all Acragas, indeed, one of the best-preserved Doric temples in the entire Greek world,

---

9   Rupe Atenea is a large rocky hill in Agrigento, Sicily. In ancient times, it was an important part of the Greek city of Akragas. Sitting about 351 meters above sea level, it was both a sacred place for worship and a good spot for keeping watch over the area.

the Temple of Concord. The name is a misnomer, given in later times, but the structure itself stands proud and nearly whole upon its pedestal, the very embodiment of Hellenic harmony and dignity. Erected about 440 B.C., its columns are of the purest Doric order, fluted and tapering with graceful entasis, and its entablature, though shorn of its decoration, still retains the perfect proportions of its style. This noble edifice owes its preservation to a curious accident of history: in the sixth century, a Christian bishop converted it into a basilica, embedding its colonnades within walls and thus unwittingly protecting it from the elements and the hands of time.

It is only as we walk between the golden-toned columns of this temple, with the southern sea stretching in haze beneath us and the modern city clustered on the heights beyond, that we begin to comprehend the true genius of the Greek builders, not merely in skill and measurement, but in that incommunicable sense of place, of alignment with nature and the divine. They built, not merely to house statues or hold ceremonies, but to speak to the gods through stone and sky, and the Temple of Concord still speaks, though its altars are cold and its worshippers gone.

Beyond it lie the ruins of the Temple of Hera (often called Juno), placed at the eastern extremity of the sacred ridge, overlooking the ravine where once the city's defensive walls plunged down to meet the river Akragas. This temple was perhaps among the earliest constructed here, built around 450 B.C., and though its roof and inner chamber have long since disappeared, many of its columns still stand, tall and solemn, in a silent row against the sky. Some bear black scorch-marks, said to be the relics of the fire set by the Carthaginians when they took the city, or perhaps the later ravages of earthquakes and lightning. The steps are worn by centuries of pilgrim feet, and one may still trace the stylobate's long curve as it accommodates the slope of the hill with quiet mathematical genius.

To walk through this landscape is not merely to survey ruins, but to breathe an atmosphere where nature and antiquity are entwined. Wild thyme and caper bushes grow from the cracks in the stone; lizards sun themselves upon fallen capitals. A shepherd's flute may echo from the gorge, much as it must have done two thousand years ago. There is here no artificial separation between past and present, no rope or plaque to bar the soul's communion. The dead cities of Sicily live on their hilltops, not in museums.

And so we descend from the heights, the temples receding behind us like a dream of marble and light, while in the distance the modern town of Agrigento sprawls untidily, its concrete and steel a poor heir to the marble perfection above. Yet even here, in a narrow alley or an old courtyard shaded by orange trees, the ghost of Acragas lingersl perhaps in a frieze repurposed as a doorstep, or a carving half-obscured behind plaster.

No visitor leaves this place untouched. Whether moved by the scale of the architecture, the serenity of the setting, or the melancholy grandeur of decline, one cannot help but feel that here, in these ruins open to sun and wind, something essential of the human spirit endures, its striving for order, for beauty, and for communion with the divine.

And so our journey continuesl eastward still, to explore the other great cities of Magna Graecia, where the sons of Hellas left their imprint upon the western world, and where, in sun-drenched valleys and along high ridges, the past yet breathes.

Beyond the desecrated shrine of Heracles, we pressed onward along the same ancient spine of rock, beneath a sky that seemed to burn with the same light that had once shone on those marble entablatures in their full splendor. Every step brought us closer to ruins whose names are uncertain but whose presence is no less eloquent for that. The earth here is crowded with fragments, blocks of tufa and limestone, shattered architraves, bits of fluting, the deep grooves of water-worn stylobates, each bearing witness to the grandeur and violence of time.

Soon we arrived at the so-called Temple of Castor and Pollux, or what remains of it: four columns and a ragged architrave re-erected by 19th-century hands more in hope than in accuracy. Yet these columns, whether faithful to the original or no, have about them a noble melancholy, standing solitary amid fig trees and wild fennel, like sentinels of a forgotten order. If they are not precisely as the Dioscuri saw them, still they catch the light and sky as the Greeks meant them to. The temple they commemorate must have had thirty-four such columns in all, a hexastyle of moderate size but exquisite proportions. The site itself is low, almost marshy, and perhaps a place of ritual processions or fountains, rather than of austere sacrifices on high. And thus even in its decay it conjures a different mood, less lofty, more intimate, a place for twilight hymns and floral offerings, rather than thunderous rites of war gods.

A little farther along we passed the remains of a temple thought to be sacred to Vulcan, or Hephaestus, but they are scant and broken, overgrown and half-buried in grasses and moss. Few linger there. The stones have slumped into the slope toward the river Hypsas, and no effort has been made to rescue them from forgetfulness. Yet the silence there has its own dignity, the kind that belongs to nameless dead and causes long lost. In truth, the valley of the temples is not uniform in its grandeur; some structures have been revered, restored, inscribed upon, others simply endured the centuries in mute resignation, slowly crumbling beneath the roots of almonds and under the tread of goatherds. The hand of man, once so exultant here, is now indifferent or absent.

Temples of "Castor and Pollux",
Valle dei Templi, Agrigento, Sicily, Italy
(*Author: trolvag, Wikipedia Common*)

From this vantage, as we pause, we look back along the ridge, across the scattered silhouettes of broken sanctuaries, to the towering mass of the Temple of Zeus, whose shattered bulk still commands the plain. And in that direction, too, we see what little is left of the ancient theatre, its cavea eroded and reclaimed by the fields, and near it, traces of a bouleuterion, or council hall, all but consumed by later constructions. Nature and agriculture have erased what time spared.

Yet for all this ruination, nothing here feels dead. These ruins do not expire they endure. The very earth seems to breathe of the lives once led above it: of priests anointing altars at dawn, of sculptors chiseling flutes into vast drums of stone, of traders debating grain at the agora, of boys racing in the dusty palestra. Even the silence speaks, if one listens with the inner ear.

As we turn to descend once more, the sun slipping behind the temple-studded ridge casts each broken column in long shadow. The olive trees turn silver in the breeze. Far below, the modern sprawl of Agrigento begins to glitter with electric light, so alien, and yet so close. But here above, where the gods once looked on from carved pediments and from within hollow bronze, there is only the sound of the wind, the cicadas, and the faint pulse of an old world refusing to disappear.

About three hundred yards further along the path, continuing in the same direction, we come to two of the great temples that still stand upright. For anyone encountering such a structure for the first time—one not reduced to a crumbled ruin but rising as it did in ancient times—it is a moment of profound wonder. Unlike broken remains that require imagination to reconstruct, these temples speak directly and clearly. Their harmony is immediate and undeniable. One instantly senses the beautiful law of proportion running through every line, the graceful simplicity of their form, and the deep, almost instinctive understanding of rhythm and symmetry that guided the ancient Greek builders. These qualities are so precisely and sensitively expressed in the stone that we instinctively move beyond architectural analysis, reaching instead for the language of music or poetry. We may find ourselves describing them not in technical terms but as one might a poem, a melody, an epic, or a symphon, for it is rhythm that gives structure both to music and to sacred scripture.

Standing before such works, we're also drawn to consider what they reveal about the Greek mind and spirit. Their art reflects their worldview and is inseparable from the language they spoke. The Greek word *kosmos*, for example, means both "order" and "beauty", showing how the Greeks saw these as essentially the same thing. To them, to live well was to live in harmony with this universal order. The concept of *kalokagathia* captures their belief that true beauty and moral goodness are deeply connected. Eudaimonia, their word for happiness, meant more than pleasure, it described the state of someone who lived rightly and stood well with the gods. And *aletheia*, their word for truth, meant something that could never be forgotten, something that endures. These ideas shaped their philosophy, their ethics, and clearly, their art and architecture.

There is also a powerful emotional restraint in these temples, a cool, almost impersonal majesty, that recalls the characters in ancient Greek tragedies. In those dramas, people are often driven by forces beyond their control: by fate, necessity, or the will of the gods. This same sense of inevitability and detachment seems carved into the stone. Religion was the root of both their dramatic stories and their architectural efforts, and just as their plays often share recurring themes and expressions, so too do their temples echo similar forms and patterns. Unlike the warm, human-centered emotion we find in Gothic architecture, with its expressive saints and heavenly light, classical architecture has a kind of still, abstract dignity. Ethically, the difference might be said to lie between Ananké—

the Greek goddess of Necessity and the Christian concept of "Free Will". But let us now return to the main path of our journey.

The first of these two temples is dedicated to a goddess the people of ancient Akragas were perhaps most in need of Concordia, the goddess of harmony. Her presence would have been a blessing in a city so often torn by internal strife. The history of Akragas is marked not only by foreign invasions but also by constant civil unrest and factional conflict. One might imagine that the goddess of Concord turned a deaf ear to the sweet prayers once sung to her here. While the mighty Zeus and heroic Heracles were honored with grand, sprawling sanctuaries, it was Concord who received what is arguably the most perfectly preserved and beautifully proportioned Greek temple in Sicily and possibly in all of Europe.

As serene and harmonious as its patron deity, the Temple of Concordia measures 138 feet in length and 64 feet in width. Thirty-four golden-yellow sandstone columns rise from its base, six at the front and back, eleven along each side, each tapering in graceful proportion from a circumference of fifteen feet at the base to nine feet at the top, and standing about twenty-three feet tall. Above them still rest the complete architrave and pediments, rare survivals of ancient craftsmanship. Other than the Theseion in Athens, there is no Doric temple more intact. Positioned dramatically along the ridge that served as the city's natural fortification, the temple stood as a visible appeal for peace, peace not only to invading Carthaginians and Romans, but also to the restless citizens of Akragas who gathered in the bustling agora nearby. And yet, despite this eloquent symbol of unity, peace never truly came.

Ironically, we owe the temple's survival not to its original worshippers, but to a much later era. By the time its builders and the market crowds of Akragas had long faded into history, and the agora had turned into olive groves and terraces of fig and vine, a new people arrived. They transformed the ancient sanctuary into a church, dedicating it to St. Gregory of the Turnips, a patron saint of farmers. The temple's inner chamber, the cella, remains the most complete on the island. Its side walls still show the round openings cut during its use as a Christian church. And rather than blame Christianity, as some hasty antiquarians have done, we ought to be grateful. In A.D. 399, the emperors Arcadius and Honorius ordered most pagan temples to be destroyed and repurposed for civic infrastructure: bridges, roads, and aqueducts. Only those adapted for Christian use were spared. So, if anything, we should regret that more temples weren't saved in this way. Concordia's shrine survived not just because it was beautiful, but because it was transformed and in that transformation, ironically, it found the peace its ancient city never could.

A half-mile walk farther along the ancient road brings us to the next great site. The path is bordered by the remains of Agrigento's ancient city wall, carved directly from the natural rock, a wall so prominent that even Virgil described seeing it from the sea (*Aeneid*, Bk 3). Along the inner face of this wall, time has hollowed out rows of tombs and burial niches. Once these held marble facings and urns of ashes, but now they stand empty, stripped of their memorials, silent reminders of a vanished civilization. Following this solemn stretch, we arrive at a temple traditionally, but cautiously, identified as the Temple of Juno Lacinia. It is gloriously situated at the southeastern edge of the ancient city, occupying the highest point on the limestone ridge that steps down from the heights of the Acropolis.

Italy, Sicily, Agrigento, Valley of the Temples,
Temple of Juno Lacinia

(Berthold Werner, Creative Commons Attribution-Share Alike 3.0)

Perched dramatically on the edge of a steep cliff 390 feet above sea level, the temple commands a breathtaking view of the African Sea, which lies about two and a half miles away, though it seems much closer, glittering beneath the Sicilian sun. The temple itself is built atop a high stylobate, or platform, with a grand flight of steps leading up to its eastern porch. Towering remnants of the city wall press close to its southern flank. Dating slightly earlier than the Temple of Concordia, it shares the same Doric design and general dimensions, though it is a bit smaller and not as well preserved. Of its original 34 columns, 25 remain standing, some complete, others reassembled. The southern columns, more exposed to the harsh scirocco wind that blows up from the Sahara across the Mediterranean, are visibly more worn than those on the northern side, which have weathered the centuries in better condition. Little remains of the entablature, but a portion of the pedestal that once held the statue of the goddess is still visible in the temple's central nave, along with stone seating where worshippers may have gathered to witness sacrificial rites.

There is a local tradition that sometimes refers to this building as the Temple of the Virgins. The name comes from a story about the famed painter Zeuxis, who was commissioned to create an image of Juno, queen of the gods. Seeking perfection, he is said to have selected five maidens from Girgenti (modern Agrigento) as models to compose an idealized figure. However, this story likely confuses this temple with another, possibly the temple of Juno at Croton[10], and perhaps even with

10   The Temple of Juno Lacinia is the remains of an ancient

a different subject altogether, such as a painting of Helen of Troy. Still, the legend lingers, adding a layer of poetic charm to a site already rich with myth, memory, and monumental grandeur.

These temples are lighter in proportion than those of Egesta and Selinus and are therefore probably a little later in date. Diodorus states that they were all erected by means of the money obtained by the sale of the city's olive oil at Carthage, while the captives made in B. C. 480 (about the date of the temple of Juno) at the battle of Himera provided so large a number of slaves that they were no doubt employed in this work. Some of the citizens are said to have possessed 500 slaves apiece, and by their labor the subterranean canals, the fishponds and temples would be formed; for quarrying stone was a very ready means of utilizing prison labor.

It was a saying of the ancients that the Acragentines built as if they were to live forever and feasted as if they were to die tomorrow, and we may judge for ourselves, now more than 2,000 years after, how true the first part of the epigram was. We are not likely to be able to exceed in imagination

---

Greek temple in southern Italy, near the modern town of Crotone, Calabria.

the magnificence that this terrace of cathedrals must have displayed when these temples stood fair and perfect within a few yards of each other, nor should we be satisfied with simply inspecting their remains. It is a liberal education to sit down amongst them and recall the history also of the wonderful city of which they only formed a part, and little is done if the visitor come but to mark the antithesis that the shrunken modern Girgenti presents to the mighty Acragas. We can scarcely at first realize that it was once the wonder of the island, and unless we have studied the history of the period in which it flourished we are unflushed with the enthusiasm that the scene about us should kindle.

The story of the magnificent buildings that once stood in Acragas, now modern-day Agrigento, is vividly described by the ancient historian Diodorus the Sicilian. He speaks with admiration of the city's wealth, the prosperity of its cattle-owning citizens, their abundance of statues and paintings, and the luxury and refinement of their homes. Acragas enjoyed a brief but extravagant existence, marked more by splendor than by peace. Its history is a dramatic one, full of ups and downs. Though it rose quickly in wealth and beauty, it never found lasting stability.

Founded around 582 B.C., Acragas reached
remarkable heights under the rule of Phalaris,
a tyrant infamous for his cruelty. Within just
twelve years, he had elevated the city to become
the second most important on the island of Sicily.
Yet this rapid rise was followed by moral decline,
as the city became consumed by excess and was
ultimately brought down in one of the most
devastating collapses recorded in ancient history.
Over the years, Acragas changed allegiances
multiple times, first siding with its conquerors,
only to be destroyed by Rome; then shifting
loyalty to Rome, only to be betrayed to Carthage.
In between these dramatic turns, it was plagued by
internal strife and division, reflecting a legacy as
turbulent as it was grand.

Two names will stand out in the mind of every
visitor to Girgenti (modern Agrigento): Phalaris
and Empedocles. This is not because they were
the most virtuous or the only notable figures in
the city's history, but because their stories are
the most dramatic and memorable. While few
today remember the wise ruler Theron, whose
Romanized tomb still stands outside the Golden

Ephebe of Agrigento. Sicilian Greek work of white marble imported from Greece. Between the Archaic and the Classical periods, arround 480 BC (or 470 BC). Finding in cistern at the area of San Biagio, near the Demeter Temple in Akragas (Agrigento). Archaeological Museum of Agrigento. (Zde: Creative Commons Attribution)

Gate of the city—nearly every schoolchild knows the gruesome tale of Phalaris and his brazen bull, and the legendary leap of the philosopher Empedocles into Mount Etna. It is unfortunate that Phalaris's reputation for cruelty has so overshadowed a fair assessment of his political skill. In truth, it was largely due to his leadership that Acragas rose swiftly to such power and splendor. The modern misuse of the word "tyrant" often implies only oppression, yet in ancient Greek political language, a tyrant was simply someone who seized absolute power outside of the usual constitutional framework. Many such rulers were capable and even just.

The cruel legacy of Phalaris has, perhaps unfairly, come to define the image of tyranny itself. Modern historians, always eager either to exonerate villains or to demystify heroes, have questioned the veracity of the famous story of the brazen bull. Still, as with many ancient legends, deeper investigation often reinforces rather than disproves traditional accounts. We are once again told to take the tale seriously. The poet Pindar, writing just eighty years after Phalaris's fall, would have been unlikely to refer to the bull had it not already been well known. In his *Pythian Odes*, he condemns Phalaris in vivid terms:

"Phalaris with blood defiled,
His Brazen Bull, his torturing flame,
Hand o'er alike to evil fame
In every clime."
(*Pyth. I*, trans. Cary)

Eventually, the brazen bull was taken to Carthage by the conquerors of Acragas, but it was later returned by Scipio Africanus. According to Cicero, Scipio remarked that the Acragantines should reflect on whether it was better for the Sicilians to live under their native rulers or under Roman authority, given that this gruesome device stood as a symbol of the cruelty of their former leaders and the clemency of Rome. (Verres, V. xxxiii.) However, the comparison rings rather hollow, especially considering that Cicero made it while denouncing Verres, a Roman governor notorious for his greed and sacrilege, hardly a glowing example of Roman generosity.

The Brazen Bull of Phalarus
Pierre II Woeiriot de Bouzey
Artist, French, 1532 – 1599,
(National Gallery of Art, Washington DC)

The Castle of Licata, once the ancient city of Phintias, was called Ecnomos the Monstrous, as it was believed to have housed the bull. Today, the figure is said to lie beneath the sea, having been cast into its depths. The tale, however, lives on. Sicilian peasants recall it as vividly as English schoolboys do, and it often decorates the sides of traditional Sicilian carts. One side may show Perillus being thrown into the brazen bull with Phalaris nearby, while other panels might depict sacred stories, a ballet scene, or King Roger battling the Arabs. The punishment itself, so alien to typical Greek customs, may reflect an influence of Phoenician cruelty. In it, we might trace echoes of the bull of the Herculean Melkart and the fiery rites of Moloch. High on the acropolis, beneath the Church of Santa Maria dei Greci, stand the columns of Acragas's most ancient temple, possibly the very place where Phalaris once offered sacrifices to Zeus of the Atabyrian hill of Rhodes, while, far off at Ecnomos, the cries of his victims echoed in the air.

We have little modern experience that allows us to truly bring the figures of ancient despots to life, the awe they inspired, the fear they commanded, and the drama of their reigns are lost to us. As a result, our attempts to imagine them moving among the crowds of the ancient city, in its streets and temples, are likely exaggerated and over-coloured by our imagination. However, the presence of the philosopher Empedocles, the disciple of the "long-haired Samian" Pythagoras, is easier to grasp. Portions of his writings survive, along with vivid descriptions of his influence. He appears as a poet, philosopher, naturalist, physician, and philanthropist, yet also as a man consumed by vanity, which has led many to question whether his wisdom outweighed his showmanship. Roman disdain for Greek culture may have fed this scepticism, as the more pragmatic Romans, limited by political bias and perhaps less attuned to metaphysical ideas, often dismissed such figures. Local tradition holds that Empedocles advised cutting through the crest of the great wall of rock connecting the Acropolis with the Rupe Atenea, allowing the cool northern Tramontana wind to reach the city and drive out the malaria caused by stagnant southern air, an early application of what we'd now call public health.

We can imagine Empedocles in flowing purple robes, his head crowned with Apollo's laurel, and his feet clad in sandals of saffron or even gold, speaking with passion and poetic clarity to the attentive citizens of Acragas. Sitting within the sunlit precincts of a temple, he might have captivated his audience by weaving insights from the natural world into moral and philosophical guidance. In the opening of his work *Catharma*, where he advocates moral conduct as the highest form of medicine, we glimpse the vanity that mars his legacy: "An immortal god and no longer a mortal man," he declares, "I wander among you, honored by all, adorned with the priestly diadem and blooming garlands. Into whatever famous town I enter, men and women do me reverence... some drawn to know the future, others tormented by long and terrible disease, waiting to hear the spells which will soothe suffering." And so, by the cruel irony of fate, it is the flaws of both Phalaris and Empedocles, the cruelty of one, the conceit of the other, that history has most vividly remembered. Even in seeking a dramatic end, Empedocles is said to have desired to vanish from the world in such a way that he might be thought divine. As Lucian recounts, and Milton echoes in *Paradise Lost*:

"he, to be deemed /

A god, leaped fondly into Ætna flames."

But the very cauldron into which he flung himself punished his pride—by casting out one of those elegant sandals he had so proudly worn. It was this small, telling detail that betrayed the truth of his fate.

"Deus immortalis haberi
Dum cupit Empedocles, ardentem frigidus
Aetnam
Insiluit."
Horace, *Ars Poetica*, 464

(*"Empedocles, eager to be thought an immortal god, coldly leapt into the blazing Aetna."*)

In the modern town of Girgenti, just three or four miles from the ancient temples, there is little to detain us long. It occupies only the site of the ancient Acropolis, though the views from its heights are wonderfully beautiful and deeply inspiring. Its present population is roughly equal to that of its old rival, Syracuse[11], about 22,000,

---

[11]   It may have been 22,000 in 1901, but today Syracuse (Siracursa) has a population of 120,000.

but in their prime, each city boasted as many as half a million inhabitants. The current number is some 300 fewer than the prisoners taken by the Romans during the final siege in 262 B.C., yet children swarm everywhere. Girgenti is said to have the most prolific population in all of Italy, or at least on the island. Fazzello even records an Agrigentine woman who bore seventy-three children in thirty births.[12]

Many of the townspeople now labor in the sulphur works, yet one still senses the enduring love of agriculture that characterized the first Dorian settlers, a solid, simple devotion to the land. But above all, what lingers in memory is the magnificent panorama, and the visions it evokes as evening falls and the sun sinks behind western Lilybaeum, Drepanum, and Eryx. In that reflective glow, the senses are touched by a kind of reverie. We repopulate these Libyan waters, the deserted Agora, and the silent temples; and from the Rock of Athena, we gaze once more over Girgenti la magnifica.

---

12 Tommaso Fazello, a 16th-century Sicilian historian, record-ed an Agrigentine woman bearing seventy-three children in thirty births originates from his seminal work, *De Rebus Siculis Decades Duae,* first published in Latin in 1558.

Next is Syracuse, the greatest of the Sicilian Greek cities, home of Archimedes, Theocritus, and one of the finest Greek theatres extant?

Founded by Corinthian settlers in 734 BC, Syracuse, originally Syrakousai, quickly rose to prominence as one of the most powerful and culturally rich city-states of the ancient Greek world. By the 5th century BC, it rivaled Athens in its intellectual and artistic achievements. Philosophers such as Plato walked its streets; mathematicians like Archimedes called it home. But beyond its contributions to thought and science, Syracuse was a city of sacred architecture, a place where the gods were honored in spectacular style.

The temples built in Syracuse during its Greek period are not only testaments to religious devotion but also masterpieces of Doric and Ionic architecture. Today, these ruins stand as some of the most evocative and picturesque sites in Sicily, inviting visitors to marvel at their enduring beauty and historical significance.

Begin your exploration with the Temple of Apollo, believed to be the oldest Doric temple in Sicily, dating back to the early 6th century

BC. Located in the heart of the modern city on the island of Ortygia, this temple marks the beginning of monumental stone architecture in the Western Greek world.

The Temple of Apollo in Syracuse

(Wikipedia Commons)

Though time and conquests have reduced it to fragments, the temple's remnants speak volumes. Massive column, some still standing, others collapsed, suggest the grandeur of its original form. Interestingly, the structure has served many purposes over the centuries: it was a Byzantine church, later a mosque under Arab rule, and eventually a Norman church. Each transformation adds a layer to its history, making it a symbol of Syracuse's enduring spirit and cultural diversity. The Temple of Apollo is more than just ruins; it's an emblem of the city's transformation across civilizations. Even in its partial state, the structure retains a solemn dignity, especially when bathed in the golden light of the Sicilian sun.

The Temple of Athena (Duomo di Siracusa) A short walk from the Temple of Apollo takes you to one of the most astonishing examples of ancient Greek architecture seamlessly incorporated into a Christian context: the Cathedral of Syracuse, or Duomo di Siracusa. What appears today as a Baroque cathedral was originally the Temple of Athena, built in the 5th century BC to honor the goddess of wisdom and war.

The transformation of this temple into a cathedral is a brilliant fusion of classical and Christian elements. Walk through its nave, and you'll see original Doric columns from the ancient temple still supporting the structure. These columns, worn smooth by centuries of touch and devotion, provide a direct physical link to antiquity. Behind the grandeur of the cathedral's ornate façade lies the soul of an ancient Greek sanctuary, where Athenians once offered prayers and sacrifices.

The juxtaposition of ancient pagan and later Christian architecture creates a powerful emotional resonance. It is a sacred space that has evolved with its city, bearing witness to conquest, faith, and cultural synthesis.

The 5th century BC Doric temple of Athena, Syracuse, Sicily, transformed into a Christian church during the Middle Ages.

(Author: Urban, Wikipedia Commons)

While less well known than the temples of Apollo and Athena, the Sanctuary of Demeter and Kore is a site of deep historical and religious significance. Located near the edge of Ortygia, this sanctuary was dedicated to the goddesses of agriculture and the underworld, a reflection of Sicily's ancient ties to the myth of Persephone, who was said to have been abducted from the island by Hades.

The sanctuary, carved directly into the rock, is more humble and intimate than the grand temples, but it offers an extraordinary sense of connection to ancient ritual practices. Archaeological findings suggest it was a place for mystery rites, with votive offerings, inscriptions, and terracotta figurines left behind by worshipers.

Visiting this site evokes a quieter, more contemplative mood, contrasting the monumental grandeur of the other temples. It's a place where one can feel the earthbound side of Greek spirituality, the devotion to fertility, the seasons, and the unseen forces of life and death.

Although technically just outside the ancient core of Ortygia, the Archaeological Park of

Neapolis is an essential part of Syracuse's Greek heritage. Within this expansive area lies the Greek Theatre of Syracuse, one of the largest and most impressive of the ancient world. Carved directly into the limestone hillside, this theater could once seat over 15,000 spectators and hosted plays by Aeschylus and Euripides.

Archaeological Park of Neapolis - aerial view

(Agostino Sella, Wikipedia Commons)

While not a temple, the Greek theatre holds a deeply religious dimension, it was closely tied to Dionysus, the god of wine and drama.

Festivals in his honor included performances that were both entertainment and spiritual observance. Standing at the top tiers of this vast amphitheater, you can look out over the city and the sea, feeling the same awe and wonder that inspired ancient audiences over two millennia ago.

Nearby, you'll also find the Altar of Hieron II, one of the largest known sacrificial altars from antiquity, believed to have been used for mass animal sacrifices during public ceremonies. These massive structures underscore the importance of religion in public life and the central role Syracuse played in the Greek Mediterranean.

Most of the major temple sites in Syracuse are open year-round, with easy access from the city's central areas. The Duomo di Siracusa continues to function as a church, and entry is typically free outside of special events. The Temple of Apollo is visible in the open air and requires no ticket to visit.

The Archaeological Park of Neapolis requires an entry ticket, but the fee includes access to the Greek Theatre, the Roman Amphitheatre, and other fascinating ruins.

For the best experience, consider hiring a local guide or taking an audio tour that contextualizes what you see with the myths, history, and political drama of ancient Syracuse. Sunset visits, especially to the Temple of Apollo and the Greek Theatre, offer not only cooler temperatures but a truly magical atmosphere.

The Greek temples of Syracuse are more than relics of a distant past, they are living memories etched in stone, part of a city that continues to thrive while honoring its ancient soul. Whether you're a history enthusiast, a lover of art and architecture, or a curious traveler drawn to the beauty of the Mediterranean, Syracuse offers a profound and moving connection to the world of Ancient Greece.

Wandering through its ancient sanctuaries, you may find yourself walking alongside philosophers, priests, and poets, each whispering through the ruins that the sacred never truly fades. It transforms, endures, and continues to inspire.

(END)

From Theocritus' Idyll VII
(The Harvest Home)

(translated/adapted from the Greek)

Where Etna lifts her wreath of snow
Above the laughing fields below,
There, Pan and shepherds pipe at noon,
And olives dream beneath the moon.

Sweet are the bees that hum through thyme,
Sweet are the boys that sing in time,
And sweetest still, the sea-wind's tune
Along the shores of fair Megara.

O Sicily, my mother mild,
Nurse of the grape and country child,
I'll sing no song more dear to me
Than these green slopes beside the sea.

CONNOR COURT TITLES CELEBRATING ITALIAN CULTURE IN ITALY AND ABROAD

Diaspora Parliaments:
How Australia Faced the Italian Challenge

Bruno Mascitelli, Rory Steele & Simone Battiston

Examines how Italian expatriates in Australia and Italian legislation affected Australian policy and identity.

Enemy Aliens:

The Internment of Italian Migrants in Australia During the Second World War

Cate Elkner, Ilma Martinuzzi O'Brien, Gaetano Rando and Anthony Cappello

A collection of essays on the wartime internment of Italian-Australians.

Il Globo:

Fifty Years of an Italian Newspaper in Australia

Edited by Bruno Mascitelli & Simone Battiston

Traces the history of the Italian-language newspaper Il Globo in Australia, its cultural role and community presence.

Italy and Australia:
An Asymmetrical Relationship

Edited by G. Cresciiani & Bruno Mascitelli

A collection of essays exploring the political, social and cultural relations between Italy and Australia.

Letters to Naples:
A Neapolitan Writes Home about his Work in Melbourne 1919-1928

Vincenzo De Francesco SJ

First-person letters of an Italian Jesuit in Melbourne in the early 20th century, providing insight into the Italian community of that time.

Great Rivalries
Cycling and the Story of Italy

Kevin Andrews

Foreword by Simon Gerrans

A sport-cultural history of cycling in Italy, and how it reflects and shaped modern Italy.

www.connorcourtbooks.com.au

www.ingramcontent.com/pod-product-compliance
Lightning Source LLC
Chambersburg PA
CBHW060055100426
42742CB00014B/2848